Toadstool Town

BY SONJA-MARIA MATTILA, MYCOLOGIST
& HK

Welcome to toadstool town....
A tiny world, unseen by most.

I bet you didn't know, the real magic...

takes place on the forest floor.

Ancient, very old beings, of long, long before our time.

The citizens of Toadstool Town...

Mushrooms.

However, in this town...
not only mushrooms, but
everyone has to play a part.

From the tiniest insect...

to the tallest bear.

A FRIENDLY TOAD

Even underground big things are brewing!

Mushrooms have a big heart...

...they share food and news with everyone.

Underground, everything is connected!

A MUSHROOM, THE FRUIT OF THE FUNGUS

MYCELIUM, THE MAIN BODY OF THE FUNGUS

PLANT ROOTS

A SUSPICIOUS TOAD

Some mushroom webs are connected to the roots of trees. Sharing nutrients with them, and helping them grow large and strong.

Some of the residents in toadstool town are Invisible... to the human eye.

bacteria, viruses, fungi and nematodes live together in the soil.

A MUSHROOM CAP

But not all of them are friends.

Fungi and bacteria have been at war for centuries!

THE FLY AGARIC
(AMANITA MUSCARIA)

THE ENGLISH NAME

THE SUPER SMART NAME

Let's explore all the neighborhoods...

...of Toadstool Town.

VERY POISONOUS FOR HUMANS.
SOME ANIMALS ENJOY TO EAT IT, MAKE A
HOME OUT OF IT OR JUST DANCE AND JUMP
AROUND IT BECAUSE IT LOOKS SO PRETTY

WHEN YOU SEE A SKULL IT
MEANS THE MUSHROOM IS
POISONOUS FOR HUMANS

Here lives the Amanita family. Always near a conifer tree.

PANTHER CAP
(AMANITA PANTHERINA)

DESTROYING ANGEL
(AMANITA BISPORIGERA)

BOTH ARE POISONOUS FOR HUMANS LIKE MANY AMANITA MUSHROOMS. MANY ARE FRIENDS WITH TREES, CONNECTING TO THEIR ROOTS - THAT'S CALLED A SYMBIOSIS!

THE HORN OF PLENTY
(CRATERELLUS CORNUCOPIOIDE)

Chanterelles, the perfect spot to hide from hungry owls!

A VERY DELICIOUS MUSHROOM TO EAT BUT IT IS HARD TO FIND. THEY HIDE UNDER FALLEN LEAVES AND THEY ALSO LOOK LIKE BROWN WRINKLED LEAVES.

WHEN YOU SEE A POT NEXT TO A MUSHROOM IT MEANS YOU CAN COOK AND EAT IT

THE GOLDEN CHANTARELLE
(CANTHARELLUS CIBARIUS)

or to knit a
pair of
socks...

...hmm, where
did the other
sock go?

ONE OF THE MOST WANTED
MUSHROOMS, NOT ONLY BECAUSE IT
TASTES SO GREAT BUT ALSO
BECAUSE IT IS SUPER HEALTHY!

PORCINI
(BOLETUS EDULIS)

The boletes are a sort of celebrity in our town...

THE UNDERSIDE OF A BOLETE MUSHROOM CAP LOOKS JUST LIKE A SPONGE! IT IS A DELICACY WORLDWIDE.
CONIFERS ARE ITS FAVORITE TREE.

Usually, it's all about them.

ORANGE BIRCH BOLETE
(LECCINUM VERSIPELLE)

MOTTLED BOLETE
(LECCINUM VARIICOLOR)

THESE ARE A BIT DIFFERENT COLORED BOLETES BUT DO NOT WORRY! THEY ARE EDIBLE. THE BIRCH IS THE FAVORITE TREE OF AN ORANGE BIRCH BOLETE.

TRUE MOREL
(MORCHELLA)

In this part of the town...
... bees gather.

MORELS ARE VERY DELICIOUS AND THEY ARE SOLD ON MARKETS. THEY LOOK LIKE HONEYCOMBS. BE CAREFUL... THE FALSE MOREL LOOKS VERY SIMILAR BUT IS POISONOUS!

TRUFFLES
(TUBERACEAE)·

TRUFFLES ARE MUSHROOMS THAT GROW UNDERGROUND. THEY ARE VERY VERY DELICIOUS AND EXPENSIVE. PIGS AND DOGS CAN BE TRAINED TO LOOK FOR THEM.

Uh oh... this little fellow thinks his poop ball is a truffle.

Oopsie daisy.

THE PARASOL MUSHROOM

(MACROLEPIOTA PROCERA)

YOU CAN COAT AND FRY THE CAP OF THE PARASOL MUSHROOM LIKE A STEAK. BUT IT IS EASY TO MISTAKE IT FOR A VERY POISONOUS MUSHROOM.

THE UPRIGHT CORAL MUSHROOM
(RAMARIA STRICTA)

THE CORAL FUNGUS IS SUPER FUNNY-LOOKING! THEY COME IN MANY DIFFERENT COLORS SUCH AS YELLOW, ORANGE, RED AND VIOLET. IT IS NOT VERY TASTY.

SAFFRON MILK CAP
(LACTARIUS DELICIOSUS)

MILK CAPS ARE FRIENDS WITH MANY DIFFERENT TREES AND THEY LEAK MILK WHEN YOU BREAK THEIR SURFACE... BUT NOT COW'S MILK!

OYSTER MUSHROOM
(PLEUROTUS OSTREATUS)

CAN YOU IMAGINE? OYSTER MUSHROOMS EAT TINY WORMS! THEY ARE ALSO VERY GOOD AT SUCKING HARMFUL METALS AND OILS FROM THE SOIL.

SHIITAKE
(LENTINULA EDODES)

SHIITAKE IS A VERY FAMOUS FOOD MUSHROOM. IT IS SUPER HEALTHY AND IT GROWS ON OLD WOOD.

SHELF FUNGI
(POLYPORALES)

SHELF FUNGI ARE ALSO CALLED CONKS. MANY OF THEM ARE VERY TASTY, BUT ALSO CHEWY AND HARD. THEY GROW ON TREES WITHOUT STEMS, THAT'S WHY THEY LOOK LIKE SHELVES...

SHAGGY INK CAP
(COPRINUS COMATUS)

THE SHAGGY INK MUSHROOM MELTS AND CREATES INK LIKE AN OCTOPUS. YOU CAN STILL EAT THE YOUNG MUSHROOMS BUT THE OLD ONES YOU BETTER LEAVE FOR THE LITTLE BUGS.

PUFFBALL
(LYCOPERDON PERLATUM)

"PFFZZZZ"

PUFFBALLS RELEASE A SMOKE CLOUD WHEN YOU STEP ON THEM. THIS IS WHY THEY ARE ALSO CALLED WOLF'S FARTS. THE YOUNG ONES ARE EDIBLE, BUT THE OLDER ONES YOU BETTER LEAVE FOR THE LITTLE BUGS.

BIOLUMINESCENT MUSHROOMS

THESE MUSHROOMS GLOW IN THE DARK!
THEY ARE USUALLY FOUND IN THE
JUNGLE. SOME BUTTERFLIES AND INSECTS
CAN ALSO GLOW IN THE DARK.

The moss people have a very close relationship to the forest, the trees, the mushrooms, the soil, the moss, the lichen, and the insects.

lichen gallery

During the day they hide... but as the sun goes down they come out to harvest their mushrooms.

For this, they need help from their little glowing friends.

WELCOME TO OUR MOSS GALLERY. MOSSES COVER OUR FOREST FLOOR, OFFERING ALL OUR LITTLE INSECTS A SAFE HOME. DEER AND MOOSE LOVE TO SNACK ON IT!

HAVE YOU EVER NOTICED HOW MANY DIFFERENT KINDS THERE ARE? SOME OF THEM ARE RED BUT MOSTLY THEY ARE DIFFERENT GREENS. THEY ARE SO SOFT TO WALK ON!

MOSS DOESN'T HAVE ROOTS LIKE PLANTS AND THAT IS WHY IT CAN GROW ALSO ON TREES AND STONES!

STAR MOSS

APPLE MOSS

ELF-CAP MOSS

BONFIRE MOSS

HAIRCAP MOSS

PEAT MOSS

FUNGI FORM DEEP AND LONG FRIENDSHIPS WITH MANY OTHER SPECIES. ONE OF THESE SPECIES IS ALGAE, ALGAE ARE TINY LIVING BEINGS, PLANTS, THAT CAN CREATE OXYGEN. SOME FUNGI ARE ALSO VERY SMALL AND THEY GET ALONG VERY WELL.
FUNGI PROVIDE A SAFE STRUCTURE FOR ALGAE TO GROW ON AND IN RETURN, THE ALGAE PRODUCES FOOD FOR THE FUNGUS.

TOGETHER THEY FORM A WHOLE NEW LIVING BEING CALLED LICHEN!

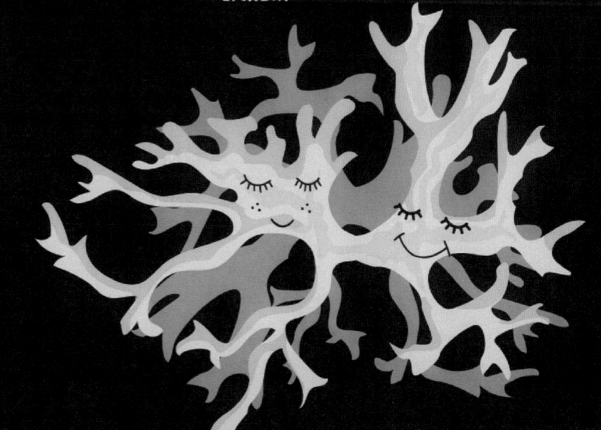

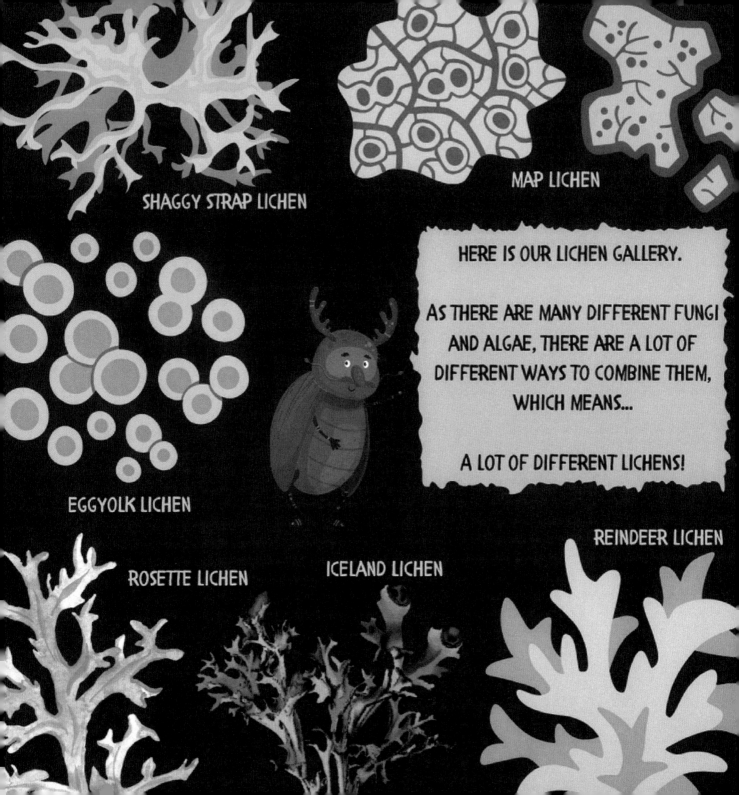

SHAGGY STRAP LICHEN

MAP LICHEN

EGGYOLK LICHEN

HERE IS OUR LICHEN GALLERY.

AS THERE ARE MANY DIFFERENT FUNGI AND ALGAE, THERE ARE A LOT OF DIFFERENT WAYS TO COMBINE THEM, WHICH MEANS...

A LOT OF DIFFERENT LICHENS!

ROSETTE LICHEN

ICELAND LICHEN

REINDEER LICHEN

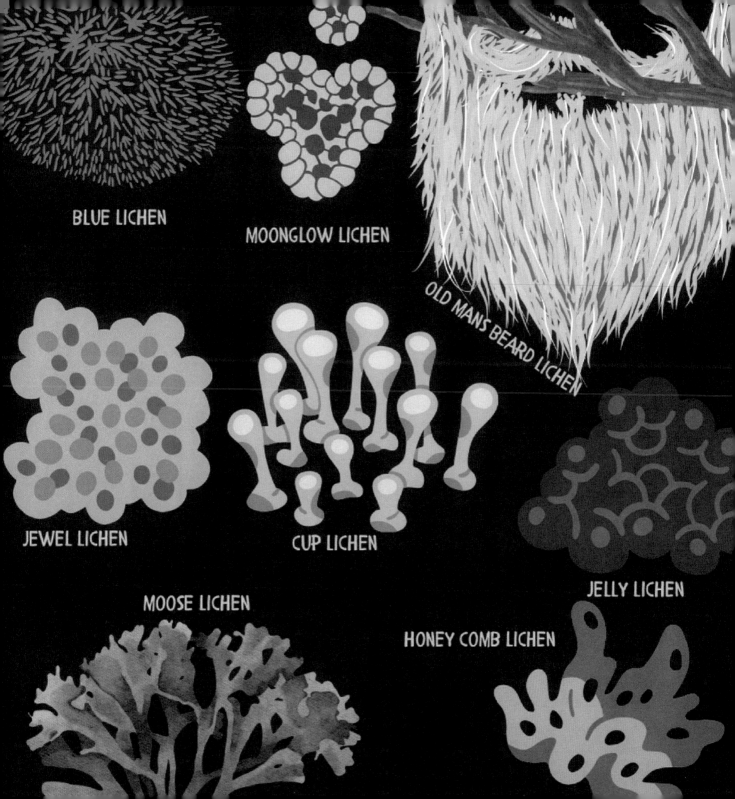

BLUE LICHEN

MOONGLOW LICHEN

OLD MANS BEARD LICHEN

JEWEL LICHEN

CUP LICHEN

JELLY LICHEN

MOOSE LICHEN

HONEY COMB LICHEN

A very old legend tells of mushrooms, that grow in circles. Such a circle is called a fairy ring.

If you were to step into that ring at a full moon, and dance the secret dance...

You will be transported into the fairy realm.

Before and after the winter animals come together and feast on the delicious mushroom treats.

MANY ANIMALS LOVE TO EAT MUSHROOMS BECAUSE THEY ARE VERY NUTRITIOUS AND RICH IN VITAMINS AND OTHER HEALTHY STUFF!

SOME ANIMALS CAN EAT MUSHROOMS THAT ARE POISONOUS TO HUMANS.

CAN YOU RECOGNIZE ALL THE ANIMALS HERE? DO YOU THINK ALL OF THEM WOULD LIKE TO EAT MUSHROOMS?

In autumn, our berries
make for a fantastic
sweet treat.

Some fungi befriend berry bushes, making them grow larger and juicier!

With these super berries, they will surely make it through the winter.

Well fed and tired
after a busy
harvesting season...

...we all deserve a good nap.

Made in the USA
Las Vegas, NV
21 December 2023

83267994R00029